Test Your Vocabulary 1

Test Your
Vocabulary 1

Peter Watcyn-Jones
and Olivia Johnston

PENGUIN ENGLISH

Pearson Education Limited
Edinburgh Gate
Harlow
Essex CM20 2JE, England
and Associated Companies throughout the world.

ISBN 978-0-582-45166-7

Eighth impression 2008
First published 1980
This edition published 2002
Text copyright © Peter Watcyn-Jones 1980, 2002
Text copyright © Olivia Johnston 2002

Designed and typeset by Pantek Arts Ltd, Maidstone, Kent
Test Your format devised by Peter Watcyn-Jones
Illustrations by Rupert Besley, Martin Fish, Bob Harvey, Val Hill and Vince Silcock
Printed in China. SWTC/08

Acknowledgements
To Dagmar Hellstam and Joy McKellen without whom there would not have been a
Test Your Vocabulary series to revise.

Published by Pearson Education Limited in association with Penguin Books Ltd, both
companies being subsidiaries of Pearson plc.

For a complete list of the titles available from Penguin English please visit our
website at www.penguinenglish.com, or write to your local Pearson Education office
or to: Marketing Department, Penguin Longman Publishing, Edinburgh Gate,
Harlow, Essex CM20 2JE.

Contents

To the student

This book will help you to learn new English words while having fun at the same time. Many of the tests use pictures – such as the tests on the weather, food and drink, jobs, clothes and parts of a house. Others are based on word types – for example, verbs, adjectives and prepositions. There are also tests on rhyming words, words that sound the same and words that people often mix up. Use the contents list to find the right test for you. Or go through the book and choose one that looks interesting or has drawings that you like. So if you feel like doing a crossword, choose a crossword. If you feel like looking at cartoons, try one of the *What are they saying?* tests where you match words to a picture. If a test is fun to do, this is one of the best ways of learning new words fast. There's no need to start at the beginning and work through every test in the book. The tests at the end are no more difficult than the ones at the beginning.

There are tip boxes on nearly every page. They will give you extra help and information. They will also give you ideas on how to learn new words.

To really **learn** a new word, you will need to do each test more than once. So use a pencil to write the answers in the book when you test yourself. Then, check your answers and look carefully at the words you didn't know or got wrong. Finally, rub out your answers ready for the next time you try that test. Each test will take you between five and fifteen minutes the first time you do it, but the next time you will probably be much quicker.

The tests in this book do not get harder as you go from Test 1 to Test 60. However, the five books in the *Test Your Vocabulary* series are carefully graded from Book 1 (for beginners) to Book 5, which is for advanced students. If you find this book is too easy, try the next one in the series.

Good luck with learning the words in this book. And we hope that you will enjoy using the words in real situations once you've learnt them here.

Peter Watcyn-Jones and Olivia Johnston

1 Missing verbs

Write the missing verbs in the sentences below. Choose from the following:

cry	~~dance~~	drink	drive	laugh	listen	put	read
run	sing	sleep	study	swim	want	write	

1   Alice and Max are learning to _____*dance*_____ the tango.

2   We usually _____ football songs on the bus.

3   I feel tired today because I didn't _____ last night.

4   He doesn't go to the beach because he can't _____ very well.

5   I always _____ to the news on the radio in the morning.

6   Are we going to _____ to the airport or go by bus?

7   It's a really sad film. It made me _____.

8   I think I'll _____ some letters tonight.

9   Jim Carrey is so funny. He always makes me _____.

10   Don't _____ all the orange juice now. Leave some for breakfast.

11   I always _____ the newspaper before I go to work.

12   The bus is at the stop now. If we _____, we'll catch it.

13   She's not hungry. She doesn't _____ any cake.

14   I'd like to _____ medicine at college.

15   Shall I _____ the milk in the fridge?

- The *w* in *write* and the *t* in *listen* are silent. We don't say them.
- The letters *gh* can make the sound *f*.

For example: *laugh, enough*

2 Opposites: adjectives

Find the opposites of the words on the left in the square and write them down. The words go down ↓ or across →.

	Adjective	Opposite		Adjective	Opposite
1	good	_bad_	9	hot	_____
2	fat	_____	10	old	_____
3	big	_____	11	happy	_____
4	tall	_____	12	fast	_____
5	full	_____	13	high	_____
6	young	_____	14	wet	_____
7	open	_____	15	hard	_____
8	rich	_____			

C	L	O	R	O	M	B	S	O	F	B
A	D	E	W	L	S	H	O	R	L	A
W	S	A	D	D	L	O	F	E	O	D
P	S	E	M	P	T	Y	T	O	W	P
N	E	W	W	O	D	S	O	N	E	S
S	A	S	T	O	R	A	S	L	O	W
M	B	H	E	R	Y	H	I	B	L	H
A	D	O	W	C	O	L	D	A	S	I
L	E	R	S	R	E	T	H	I	N	R
L	W	T	W	C	L	O	S	E	D	E
P	O	O	R	W	O	S	T	E	F	W

This is one way of learning new words. Write ten new words on a piece of paper and put it in your pocket. Carry it with you for a few days, and look at it now and again. When you know all the words, throw the piece of paper away and write a new list.

3 The body

Write the numbers 1 to 15 next to the correct words.

arm   _12_

back   ____

bottom   ____

ear   ____

eye   ____

foot   ____

hair   ____

hand   ____

head   ____

knee   ____

leg   ____

mouth   ____

neck   ____

nose   ____

teeth   ____

- The words *foot* and *tooth* have irregular plurals. The plural of *foot* is *feet* and the plural of *tooth* is *teeth*.
- The *k* in *knee* is silent. We don't say it.

4 Prepositions 1 (place)

Look at the pictures and write the missing prepositions in the sentences opposite. Use each preposition once only.

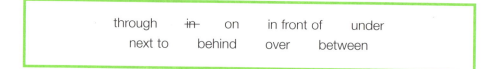

through ~~in~~ on in front of under
next to behind over between

1	The mobile phone is _____*in*_____ the bag.
2	The post office is _____ the bank and the computer shop.
3	The cat is _____ the bed.
4	The dog is lying _____ the fire.
5	He is standing _____ a tree.
6	There's a bridge _____ the river.
7	The headphones are _____ the table.
8	The cinema is _____ the restaurant.
9	They're walking home _____ the park.

Most people use the word *mobile* not *mobile phone*.

What's your mobile number?

Can you call me on my mobile, please?

In American English a *mobile phone* is a *cell phone*.

5 Missing verbs

Write the missing verbs in the sentences below. Choose from the following:

ask	carry	eat	fly	happen	hurt	kick	learn
open	~~phone~~	play	sit down	smoke	wash	watch	

1. Can you __*phone*__ the station to find out the train times?

2. The train is too slow. Let's _____ from London to Glasgow.

3. Could you _____ the window, please? It's very hot in here.

4. Did you _____ the film on television last night?

5. When did you _____ to play the guitar?

6. 'Would you like a cigarette?'
   'No, thank you. I don't _____.'

7. Could you _____ this bag, please? It's too heavy for me.

8. I'm tired. Can't we _____ for a minute?

9. I'm not going out tonight. I want to _____ my hair.

10. Don't _____ me any more questions. I'm not going to answer.

11. I've got a new computer game called *Traveller*. Do you know how to _____ it?

12. I never _____ meat. I'm a vegetarian.

13. In football you can _____ the ball or hit it with your head.

14. How did the accident _____?

15. Does your broken leg _____ a lot?

The verbs *phone*, *telephone*, *call* and *ring* all mean the same thing.

6 Food and drink 1

Write the numbers 1 to 12 next to the correct words.

a banana	_1_	fruit	_____	sausages	_____
bread	_____	an ice cream	_____	toast	_____
cheese	_____	jam	_____	vegetables	_____
a cup of tea	_____	oranges	_____	wine	_____

Château Beauvin 1998

Tea is more popular than coffee in Britain. The British drink 185 million cups of tea per day and 77% of British people drink tea regularly.

7 Family life

1 Read Charlotte's words and write the names of the people on the family tree.

'My name's Charlotte. I'm married to John. We have two children, Stephen and Sylvia. My mum's name is Theresa and my father is called Alan. I have two sisters and a brother – Emily, Rebecca and Michael. Emily's married to Craig and they have a son called Freddie and twin daughters, Lizzie and Vicky.'

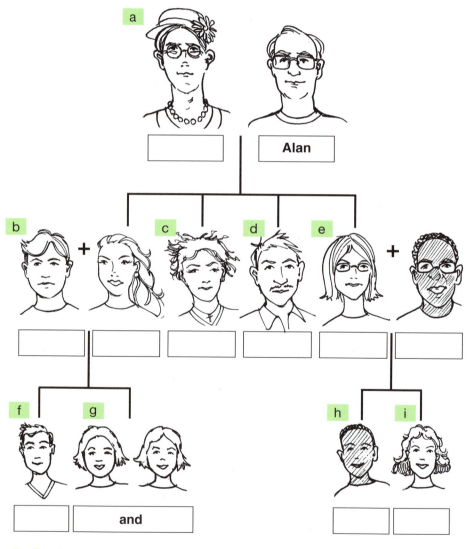

2 What do they all say about family life? Choose the correct word for each gap.

> aunt   cousin   daughter   grandchildren   granddaughter
> grandfather   grandmother   grandson   husband   mother
> nephews   nieces   parents   sisters   ~~son~~   uncle   wife

Alan: My (a) _____*son*_____, Michael, is teaching me to use a computer. I want to get on the Internet.

Theresa: It was my birthday last week. My (b) _____ Freddie made me a big chocolate cake.

Stephen: My (c) _____ Michael is great. He always buys me the best computer games.

Michael: I've got three (d) _____ and two (e) _____. Christmas is a very expensive time for me!

Craig: My (f) _____ 's family is really nice. Her (g) _____, Theresa, is great with the children.

Rebecca: Emily is always very tired. Her (h) _____, Craig, never helps her with the twins.

Sylvia: My (i) _____ Emily is quite fat.

Freddie: I hate my (j) _____, Lizzie and Vicky. They cry all the time. My (k) _____, Stephen, is cool. He's brilliant at football.

Theresa: I'm a bit worried about my (l) _____ Rebecca. She hasn't got a job or a boyfriend at the moment.

Sylvia: Both my (m) _____ wear glasses. I don't want to wear glasses when I grow up.

Freddie: My (n) _____ is called Theresa and my (o) _____ is called Alan.

Theresa: My five (p) _____ are the best thing in my life. I love those twins, Lizzie and Vicky.

Alan: My (q) _____ Sylvia is a very clever girl. She'll go far in life.

8 Missing verbs

Write the missing verbs in the sentences below. Choose from the following:

climb	~~come~~	cook	find	forget	give	keep
know	sell	shut	spell	tell	visit	walk	wear

1 Would you like to ___*come*___ to my party on Friday?

2 Excuse me, do you _____ the way to the station, please?

3 I live very near my office, so I always _____ to work.

4 Can you _____ me the name of the new student in our class?

5 Shall I _____ my blue trousers or my red skirt to Celia's party?

6 'Could you _____ your name, please?' he asked.
'L-U-C-Y. Lucy.'

7 _____ the window, please. It's cold in here.

8 Did you ever _____ trees when you were a child?

9 I think I'll _____ my car and buy a motorbike.

10 I love eating at their house. They really know how to _____.

11 We can't go by car because I can't _____ my car keys.

12 How often do you _____ your cousins in Canada?

13 Did your parents _____ you a nice birthday present?

14 You can _____ the Celine Dion CD you borrowed from me.
I don't want it.

15 I sometimes _____ my own mobile phone number!

- The *b* in *climb* and the *k* in *know* are silent. We don't say them.
- The word *walk* rhymes with *talk*.
- The vowel sound in *work* is the same as in *her*.

9 Opposites: more adjectives

Write the opposite of each word in the puzzle. What is the sentence in the darker squares?

1	interesting	6	heavy	11	clean
2	clever	7	easy	12	shallow
3	cheap	8	early	13	friendly
4	right	9	safe	14	pretty
5	quiet	10	asleep	15	kind

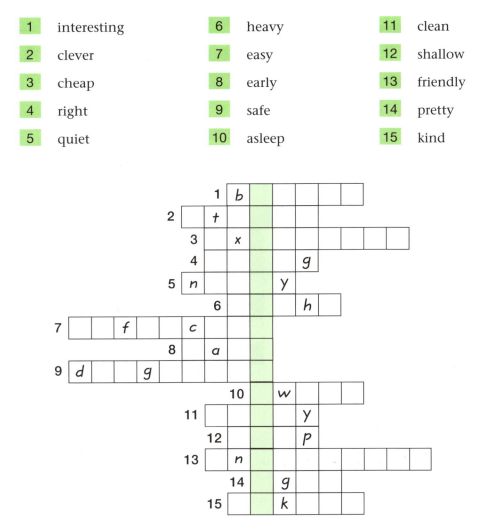

We can make the opposite of some adjectives with *-un*.

For example: *friendly / unfriendly*

interesting / uninteresting

happy / unhappy

10 Countries and nationalities crossword

Complete the crossword. Each answer is a country or a nationality.

Across

1   Mikhail was born in Russia. He is _____

3   Bettina is German. She comes from _____

4   My girlfriend is Polish. She was born in _____

7   They come from Norway. They are _____

8   Rosa is Brazilian. She comes from _____

9   Fizen is from Fethiye, in Turkey. She's _____

10 Zhang was born in China. He's _____

12 Michel was born in France. He's _____

14 Diane and Mike come from the USA. They're _____

16 Sylvie is Swiss. She's from _____

17 Dorte is Danish. She's from _____

18 They're from Sweden. They're _____

Down

2 We're Spanish. We're from _____

3 Dimitri is from Greece. He's _____

5 Keiko is from Japan. She's _____

6 Dr Fernandez is from Portugal. She's _____

8 They're British. They were born in _____

11 Roberto is Italian. He's from _____

13 They're Dutch. They're from _____

15 Dinesh comes from India. He's _____

 Write all the nationality words on this page in five groups. Can you think of any more nationality words? Add them to the correct group.

• ending in -ian / -an	• ending in -ish	• other endings
• ending in -ese	• ending in -ch	

11 Jobs 1

Choose the correct endings for the jobs: *-er*, *-or*, *-ist*. Then match the pictures to the jobs.

act *or*   ☐ 8

dent_____ ☐

doct_____ ☐

driv_____ ☐

hairdress_____ ☐

journal_____ ☐

reception_____ ☐

wait_____ ☐

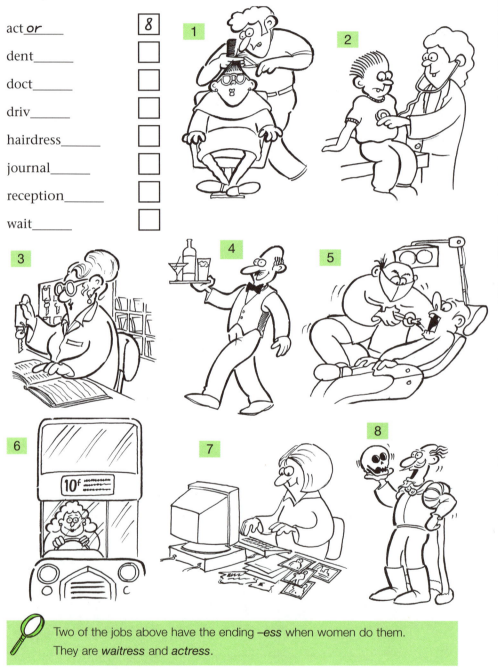

Two of the jobs above have the ending *–ess* when women do them.
They are *waitress* and *actress*.

12 Choose the word

Write the missing word(s) in each sentence.

1   My brother is very _____*tall*_____. He's 1.95 m.

(a) tall   b) high   c) long

2   My sister _____ German quite well, but I can't.

a) can   b) can speak   c) is speaking

3   My parents _____ in South Africa.

a) were born   b) are born   c) was born

4   One of my favourite sports _____ football.

a) are   b) is   c) were

5   Would you like _____ more tea?

a) some   b) little   c) have

6   How _____ is New York from Washington?

a) long   b) much   c) far

7   _____ I'm late.

a) Excuse me   b) Sorry for   c) I'm sorry

8   _____ likes John. He's very popular.

a) Everyone   b) All people   c) Nobody

9   What time do you usually _____ in the morning?

a) get up   b) sit up   c) go up

10   I didn't see you at the party, Sarah. Were you _____?

a) sore   b) bad   c) ill

13 Missing verbs

Write the missing verbs in the sentences below in the Present Simple. Before you start, read the notes in the Tip on page 17. Choose from the following:

copy   count   ~~cry~~   draw   finish   have   kill   lose
hear   help   leave   look at   speak   try   understand

1   My mother always _____ *cries* _____ when she cuts up onions.

2   She never _____ the phone because she's always got her personal stereo on.

3   What time does the next bus _____, please?

4   Laura is very clever, isn't she? She _____ six languages.

5   I always _____ the pictures in magazines before I read the stories.

6 In this game, one person _____ to a hundred and everyone else hides.

7 My girlfriend starts work at nine o'clock and _____ at five.

8 Emma always _____ my answers in Maths tests.

9 He's very good on the computer. He always _____ me if I have problems.

10 I think Josh is going to be an artist. He _____ really well.

11 Our basketball team isn't very good. We _____ nearly all our matches.

12 I don't speak German very well but I _____ quite a lot.

13 Our cat _____ a lot of birds in our garden.

14 My brother always _____ a bowl of cereal and two fried eggs for breakfast.

15 Sam _____ hard but he is really no good at football.

- In the Present Simple, the third person singular always ends in -s.
- There are spelling rules.
  Verbs ending in –y change to –ies: cry/cries.
  Verbs ending in –o, -ss, -sh, –ch, –x change to –es: go / goes, kiss / kisses, wash / washes, watch / watches, mix / mixes.
- The verb *have* is irregular. The third person singular is *has*.

14 What's the weather like?

Write what the weather is like under each picture. Choose from the following:

It's raining	It's cloudy	It's snowing	It's sunny
It's windy	~~It's freezing~~	It's foggy	It's stormy

1 _____It's freezing_____ .

2 _____ .

3 _____ .

4 _____ .

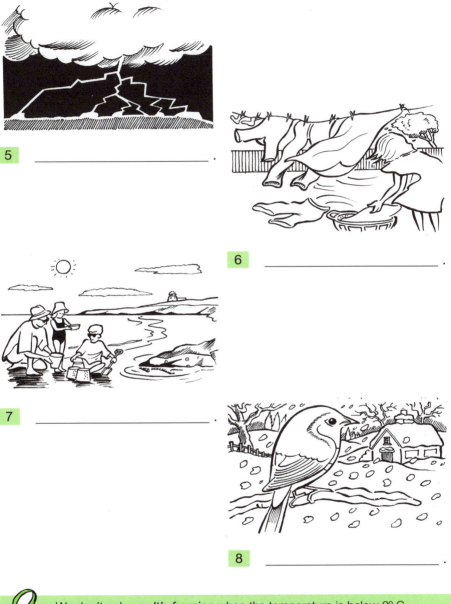

5 _____ .

6 _____ .

7 _____ .

8 _____ .

- We don't only say *It's freezing* when the temperature is below 0° C.
  It's freezing also means *It's very cold*.
- Another way of saying *It's sunny* is *The sun's shining*.

15 Fonuamotu island

1 Fonuamotu is a beautiful island. Look at the places on the map and the compass. Then complete the compass and the labels with the correct words from the box.

Airport   Beach   Bridge   East   Forest   Island   Mountains
River   Road   Sea   South   West

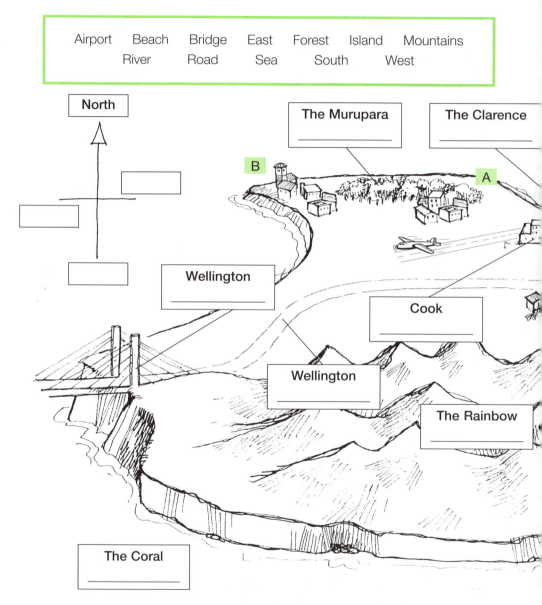

North

The Murupara
_____

The Clarence
_____

Wellington
_____

Cook
_____

Wellington
_____

The Rainbow
_____

The Coral
_____

2 Match the letters (A–E) on the map to the names of the villages.

Wellington is the village south of the airport. _____C_____

Makogai is the village between the forest and the airport. _____

Fulaga is the village north of the mountains. _____

Nacula is the village east of the river. _____

Yasawa is the village west of the forest. _____

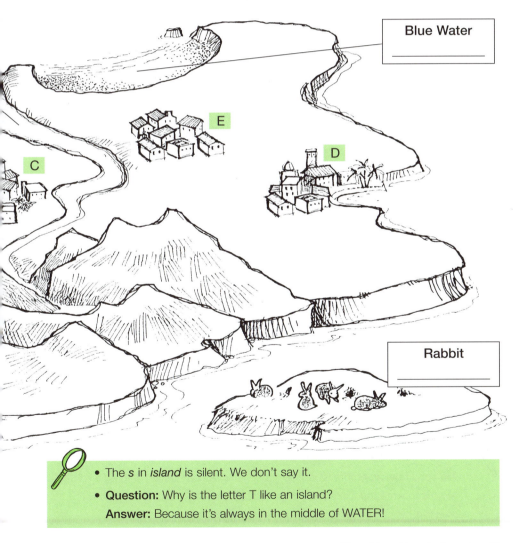

Blue Water
_____

C

E

D

Rabbit
_____

- The *s* in *island* is silent. We don't say it.

- **Question:** Why is the letter T like an island?
  Answer: Because it's always in the middle of WATER!

16 Jobs 2

Choose the correct endings for the jobs: *-er*, *-ant*, *-ian*. Then match the pictures to the jobs.

beautic*ian*____   ☐ *1*

clean_____   ☐

electric_____   ☐

optic_____   ☐

photograph_____   ☐

plumb_____   ☐

sales assist_____ ☐

teach_____   ☐

The *b* in *plumber* is silent. We don't say it.

Do you know any more words for jobs? Have a competition with a friend.
Who can write the most job words in three minutes? Then exchange lists.
You read your friend's list and your friend reads your list.

17 Plurals crossword

Complete the crossword with the plurals of the words.

Across

1	potato
3	mouse
6	foot
8	man
9	child
10	kiss
11	baby
13	taxi
14	glass

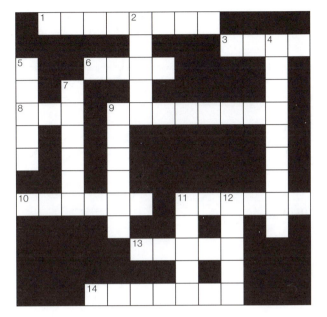

Down

2	tooth
4	country
5	woman
7	knife
9	city
11	box
12	bus

- The plural of *person* is *people*.
- The plural of *sheep* is *sheep*.
- The plural of *goose* is *geese*.

18 Food and drink 2

Write the numbers 1 to 12 next to the correct words.

apples __3__

beer _____

biscuits _____

a boiled egg _____

butter _____

a cake _____

a cup of coffee _____

meat _____

pears _____

potatoes _____

soup _____

tomatoes _____

When we talk about cake, we often use the words *piece* or *slice*.

Would you like a piece of cake?

Can I have another slice of chocolate cake?

19 Prepositions 2 (time)

Write the missing prepositions in the sentences. Use these prepositions:

<del>at</del> at at at for for in in in in in on on on

1   Let's go somewhere exciting ____at____ the weekend.

2   Would you like to come to my party _____ Friday?

3   Alice is going to Spain. She'll be away _____ three weeks.

4   I usually finish work _____ four o'clock _____ the afternoon.

5   We got to London _____ nine o'clock.

6   They got married _____ the twenty-first of August.

7   She's in the police so she often has to work _____ night.

8   We are now living _____ the twenty-first century.

9   We're going on holiday for three weeks _____ the summer.

10 She went to Italy _____ two weeks _____ July.

11 They met in Paris _____ 1982.

12 You can't go to bed early _____ New Year's Eve!

We say *in* January / August / December, but we say *on* the first / second, twenty-first of August.

20 Opposites: verbs

1 What's the opposite of each verb on the left? Choose from the verbs on the right.

	Verb	Opposite	
a	stop	_start_	take
b	laugh	_____	turn off
c	open	_____	hate
d	come	_____	borrow
e	work	_____	leave
f	bring	_____	~~start~~
g	learn	_____	answer
h	lend	_____	push
i	turn on	_____	close
j	ask	_____	teach
k	love	_____	cry
l	sell	_____	play
m	pull	_____	go
n	sit down	_____	buy
o	arrive	_____	stand up

2 Write the missing verbs in the sentences below. Choose from the verbs opposite.

a Can you _____ me to drive? I'll pay you.

b Can you _____ your CDs to my party? I haven't got many good ones.

c Don't _____ my hair. It really hurts.

d I want to _____ to play the guitar.

e I'm going to _____ all my CDs and my CD player and buy a new bike.

f Please _____ the radio. I'm trying to watch a good TV programme.

g Can you help me to _____ the car. The battery is flat and it won't start.

h 'Do you like rap music?'
'No, I don't. I really _____ it.'

When you take a video from the library for a few days, you *borrow* it.
When you give a friend a video for a few days, you *lend* it.

21 What are they saying? 1

Match the words to the pictures. Write the letters a to j in the balloons.

<table>
<tr><td>a</td><td>After you!</td><td>f</td><td>Bless you!</td></tr>
<tr><td>b</td><td>Watch out!</td><td>g</td><td>Take a seat.</td></tr>
<tr><td>c</td><td>Nice to meet you.</td><td>h</td><td>Help yourselves.</td></tr>
<tr><td>d</td><td>Excuse me, please.</td><td>i</td><td>Cheers!</td></tr>
<tr><td>e</td><td>Hold on, please.</td><td>j</td><td>I'm terribly sorry!</td></tr>
</table>

22 Missing verbs

Write the missing verbs in the sentences below in the Past Simple. Before you start, read the notes in the Tip on page 31. Choose from the following:

call   clean   cry   enjoy   invite   jump   move   need
plan   ~~rain~~   show   stop   talk   use   wait

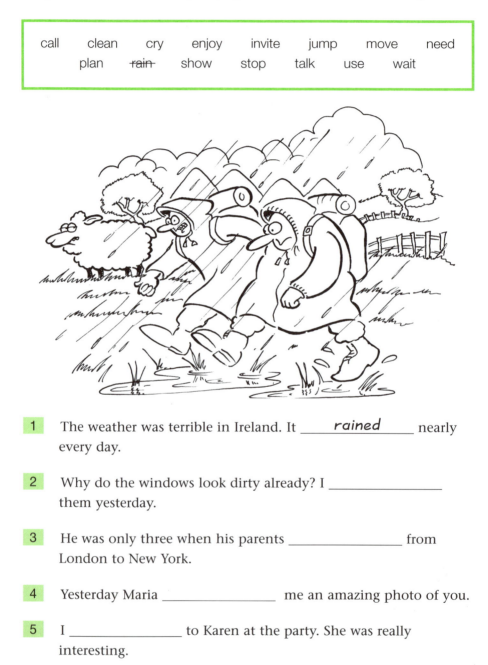

1 The weather was terrible in Ireland. It _____*rained*_____ nearly every day.

2 Why do the windows look dirty already? I _____ them yesterday.

3 He was only three when his parents _____ from London to New York.

4 Yesterday Maria _____ me an amazing photo of you.

5 I _____ to Karen at the party. She was really interesting.

6 She was really happy when she won the tennis match and she _____ over the net.

7 I _____ you three times this afternoon, but your phone was always engaged.

8 We _____ forty people to the party, but only twenty came.

9 She went to the shops because she _____ to buy some milk and eggs.

10 Thank you for a wonderful evening. I really _____ it.

11 My little sister _____ when our cat died.

12 I _____ reading that computer book because it was so boring.

13 I didn't write in pen. I _____ a pencil.

14 We _____ for you for an hour outside the cinema. Where were you?

15 They looked at the map and _____ their journey.

In the Past Simple, (positive) regular verbs end in *-ed*.
There are spelling rules.

- If the verb ends in *-e*, we add *-d*: *move / moved*.

- If the verb ends in a consonant, we add *-ed*: *show / showed*.

- If the verb ends in a consonant + *-y*, we delete the *–y* and add *-ied*: *cry / cried*.

- With some verbs ending in a consonant, we double the consonant: *stop / stopped*.

23 Food and drink 3

Write the numbers 1 to 12 next to the correct words.

beans	__4__	a glass of milk	_____	a pizza	_____
chicken	_____	a hamburger	_____	a sandwich	_____
fish and chips	_____	a hot dog	_____	spaghetti	_____
a fried egg	_____	a lemon	_____	strawberries	_____

- A *hot dog* is a sausage in a roll. People usually put *tomato ketchup* and *mustard* on their hot dog.
- *Fish and chips* are a very popular fast food in Britain.
- In English, *spaghetti* is a singular word. We say *My spaghetti is delicious.* NOT *My spaghetti are delicious.*

24 Choose the word

Write the missing word(s) in each sentence.

1 _____There's_____ a strange man outside the house.

   ⓐ There's   b) It's   c) He's

2 I _____ to Spain this summer.

   a) am going   b) think to go   c) goes

3 I usually go to _____ at 7.30.

   a) my work   b) my job   c) work

4 _____ me the salt, please.

   a) Pass   b) Take   c) Hold

5 Andy plays tennis really _____.

   a) good   b) great   c) well

6 Do you mind if Nina _____ us to the cinema tonight?

   a) comes with   b) follows   c) follows with

7 Shall we go for _____ this afternoon?

   a) a bath   b) a swim   c) swimming

8 'Oh, sorry!' '_____ '

   a) You're welcome.   b) Not at all.   c) That's all right.

9 Have you got _____ for the ticket machine?

   a) a change   b) change   c) changes

10 Can I have _____, please?

   a) a piece of bread   b) a bread   c) one bread

25 Yesterday, today, tomorrow

Look at the calendar, then complete the sentences below with words from the box.

MAY						
Mon	Tues	Wed	Thurs	Fri	Sat	Sun
		1	2	3	4	5
6	7	8	9	10	11	12
13	14	15	16	17	18	19
20	21	22	23	24	25	26
27	28	29	30	31		

this morning   tomorrow afternoon   last night   last Thursday
the day after tomorrow   this afternoon   next Thursday
~~tomorrow~~   tonight   the day before yesterday   yesterday

Today is Thursday 16th May.

1   My Canadian cousins are coming to stay _____*tomorrow*_____.
    (17th May)

2   I went to London _____. (15th May)

3   Are you going to Sally's party _____?
    (23rd May)

4 I'm going to the theatre _____. (7.30 p.m. / 16th May)

5 My sister Julia is getting married _____. (18th May)

6 I'm going to Manchester _____. (1 p.m. / 17th May)

7 Tim came to see me _____. (9th May)

8 Shall we play tennis _____? (2 p.m. / 16th May)

9 There was a good film on television _____. (8.30 p.m. / 15th May)

10 I got a letter from my brother _____. (8.30 a.m. / 16th May)

11 I bought a new car _____. (14th May)

We write dates in one way but we say them in another way.
For example, we write *Today is Thursday 16th May* but we say *Today is Thursday the sixteenth of May*.

How do we say these dates?
Monday 31st July   Tuesday 22nd March   Wednesday 3rd April

26 The house 1

Write the numbers 1 to 12 next to the correct words.

balcony __3__   gate _____   steps _____

door _____   grass _____   tree _____

garage _____   flowers _____   wall _____

garden _____   roof _____   window _____

One good way of remembering words is to make a word-web.

Choose a word or subject that you like. Write it in the middle of a big piece of paper.

Here's an example: *MUSIC*

Which words, in English or in your language, come into your head?

Use a dictionary to build a word-web like this:

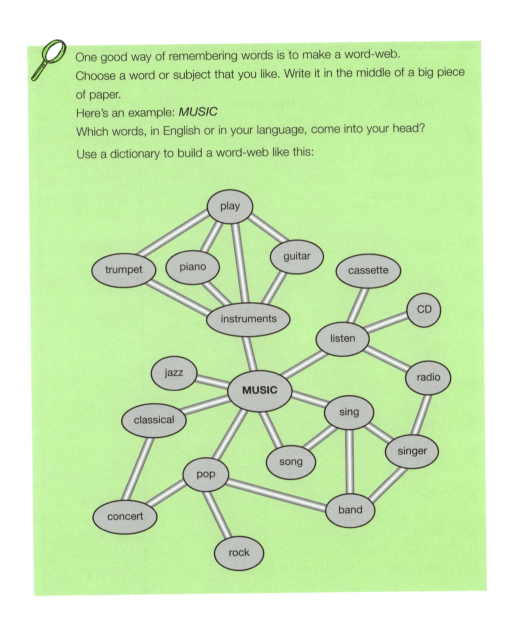

27 Opposites: more verbs

1 What's the opposite of each verb on the left? Choose from the verbs on the right.

	Verb	Opposite	
a	give	*take*	mend
b	remember		~~take~~
c	live		go to bed
d	begin		take off
e	get up		find
f	spend		finish
g	break		lose
h	put on		hide
i	win		save
j	drop		die
k	lose		whisper
l	show		go to sleep
m	wake up		pick up
n	shout		forget

2 Write the missing verbs in the sentences below. Choose from the verbs on page 38.

a I went to bed early last night but I couldn't _____ because of the noise in the street.

b I usually wake up at seven but I don't _____ until half past seven.

c Why do you always _____ your clothes on the floor at bed time? It's very untidy.

d I haven't got a pencil to write down your number but I will try to _____ it.

e I'm going to _____ a secret in your ear. I don't want anyone to hear.

f She wants to _____ up enough money to buy a video camera.

g Our team is going to _____ the match. The other team is much better.

h I hate people who _____ drink cans and sweet papers in the street.

The word *lose* has two meanings.
It means the opposite of *find*: *I often lose my glasses*.
It also means the opposite of *win*: *Our team is very good. We never lose a match*.

28 How do they look?

Look at the pictures, then write the missing words in the sentences. Choose from the following:

~~happy~~   worried   sad   tired   frightened
comfortable   ill   cold   correct   hot   embarrassed

1 She looks ___*happy*___.

2 He looks _____.

3 It looks _____.

4 He looks _____.

5 She looks _____.

6   She looks _____.

7   He looks _____.

8   It looks _____.

9   He looks _____.

10   She looks _____.

11   He looks _____.

- Another word for *frightened* is *scared*.
- Another word for **correct** is *right*.

29 Clothes 1

Write the numbers 1 to 20 next to the correct words.

boots _17_

bra _____

coat _____

dress _____

hat _____

jacket _____

jeans _____

knickers _____

pants _____

shirt _____

shoes _____

shorts _____

skirt _____

socks _____

suit _____

sweater _____

tie _____

tights _____

trainers _____

trousers _____

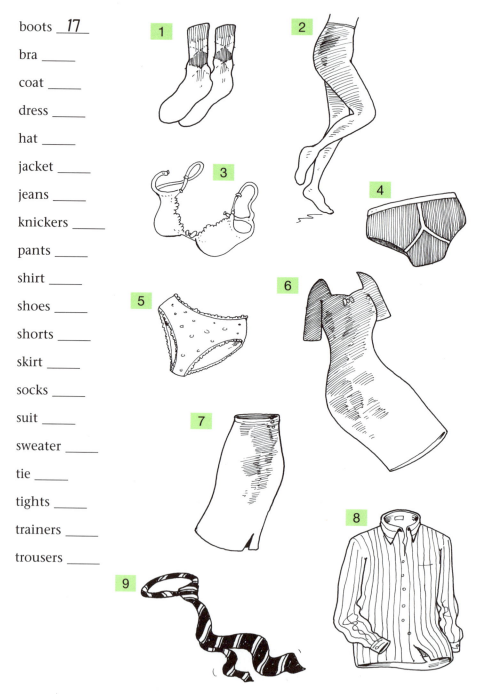

10

11

12

13

14

15

16

17

18

19

20

The words *trousers*, *jeans*, *shorts*, *tights*, *pants* and *knickers* are always in the plural.

My jeans are too tight. NOT ~~My jeans is too tight~~.

These shorts aren't comfortable. NOT ~~This shorts isn't comfortable~~.

American English *pants* = British English *trousers*.

30 Places in town 1

Write the numbers 1 to 12 next to the correct words

block of flats ___3___   museum   _____

bridge   _____   park   _____

bus stop   _____   railway station   _____

café   _____   school   _____

car park   _____   supermarket   _____

hospital   _____   traffic lights   _____

In American English a *block of flats* is an *apartment building* and a *car park* is a *parking lot*.

31 Clothes 2

Look at the pictures. What is each person wearing? Match a word from box A with a word from box B and write the correct clothes words under each picture.

A

- ballet
- baseball
- climbing
- cycling
- football
- ~~rugby~~
- skiing
- tennis

B

- boots
- cap
- hat
- helmet
- ~~shirt~~
- shorts
- skirt
- shoes

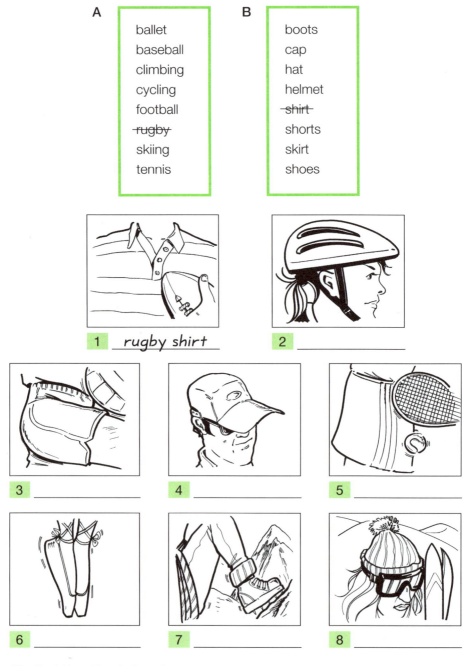

1 _rugby shirt_

2 _____

3 _____

4 _____

5 _____

6 _____

7 _____

8 _____

32 The house 2

Write the numbers 1 to 10 next to the correct words.

bathroom	2	kitchen	_____
bedroom	_____	living room	_____
dining room	_____	stairs	_____
downstairs	_____	toilet	_____
hall	_____	upstairs	_____

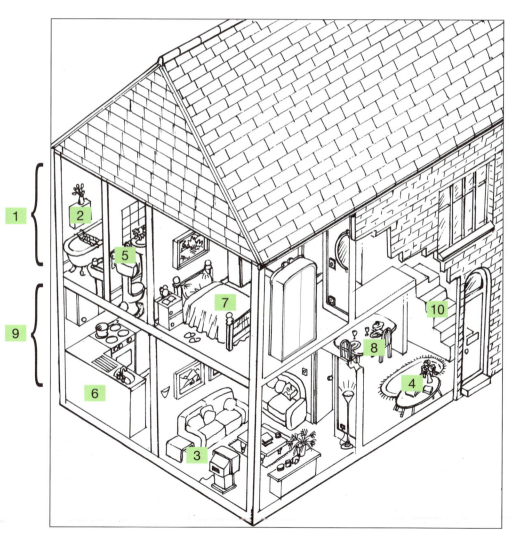

33 Prepositions 3 (mixed)

Write the missing prepositions in the following sentences.

1 I met Luigi __*at*__ a party.

    a) on   b) by   c) at

2 Sandra's going to live in Los Angeles _____ three years.

    a) for   b) during   c) by

3 Most of my friends are good _____ skiing.

    a) to   b) at   c) in

4 I live _____ Queen's Road.

    a) at   b) in   c) by

5 She's living _____ her parents until she finds a flat.

    a) in   b) by   c) with

6 Would you like a piece of cake _____ your coffee?

    a) with   b) to   c) for

7 We're having a big party _____ Tina's birthday.

    a) to   b) on   c) from

8   Shall we go _____ the cinema tonight?

a) on   b) at   c) to

9   I got a CD _____ my girlfriend _____ Christmas.

a) of / to   b) by / in   c) from / for

10   Shall we ring _____ a taxi?

a) for   b) after   c) to

11   Don't eat sweets. They're bad _____ your teeth.

a) to   b) for   c) with

12   Where's my blue purse with flowers _____ it?

a) with   b) for   c) on

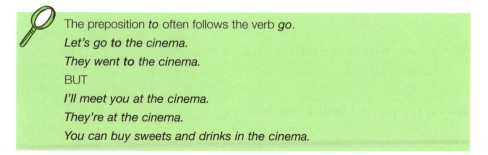

The preposition *to* often follows the verb *go*.

Let's go to the cinema.

They went to the cinema.

BUT

I'll meet you at the cinema.

They're at the cinema.

You can buy sweets and drinks in the cinema.

34 Opposites: various words

Complete each sentence with the opposite of the word in **darker type**.
Choose from the following:

> adult   after   always   bottom   country   far   future   hardly ever
> in front of   last   light   ~~nobody~~   single   worse

1   **Everybody** likes Lucy, but _____*nobody*_____ likes her boyfriend, John.

2   He lives in the **town** in the winter and in the _____ in the summer.

3   Do the exercise at the **top** of page 36 first, then the one at the _____ of page 37.

4   Are you **married** or _____?

5   Serena **never** gets up before 9.30 so I am not surprised that she is _____ late for work.

6   'Is your leg **better** now, Martin?'

'No, I'm afraid it's a lot _____.'

7   I'll carry the **heavy** suitcase and you take the _____ one.

8   I came **first** in the class in English but _____ in Geography.

9   Is the cinema **behind** the bank or _____ it?

10   Did you meet Nina **before** or _____ you left university?

11   The house is **near** the station – not _____ from the sports centre.

12   Now that I'm an _____ I wish I was a **child** again.

13   We all know what happened in the **past**, but who knows what will happen in the _____?

14   My friends **often** phone me but they _____ send me e-mails.

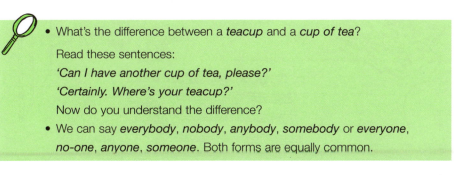

- What's the difference between a *teacup* and a *cup of tea*?
  Read these sentences:
  'Can I have another cup of tea, please?'
  'Certainly. Where's your teacup?'
  Now do you understand the difference?
- We can say *everybody, nobody, anybody, somebody* or *everyone, no-one, anyone, someone*. Both forms are equally common.

35 In the living room

Write the numbers 1 to 16 next to the correct words.

armchair	_2_	cushion	____	sofa	____
bookcase	____	light	____	television	____
carpet	____	magazines	____	vase of flowers	____
CD player	____	picture	____	video recorder	____
clock	____	remote control	____		
coffee table	____	rug	____		

36 Missing verbs

Write the missing verbs in the sentences below. Choose from the following:

> build   change   feel   hope   ~~kiss~~   lie down   mean   paint   pay
> post   recognize   repeat   smell   smile   stay

1 At the end of the film, they look into each other's eyes and
_____*kiss*_____.

2 I think I'll put a sweater on – I _____ a bit cold.

3 Is it really you, Simon? I'm sorry, but I didn't _____
you without your beard.

4 Put your money away, Tanya. I'll _____ for this!

5 Could you _____ these letters for me, please?

6 Today I helped Jade _____ her bedroom green.

7 I want to _____ my shoes. These ones are wet.

8 Are you sure it's all right to eat this fish? It doesn't
_____ very good!

9 How long did it take you to _____ your house?

10 _____ everyone! I'm going to take a photo of you.

11 You look tired. Go and _____ for a while.

12 Can you _____ that, please? I didn't hear the
question.

13 What does this word _____? It isn't in the dictionary.

14 My cousins are coming to _____ in the summer.

15 I _____ you do well in your exams.

37 What's the matter?

What does each person answer to the question *What's the matter?* Write the missing words under the pictures below. Choose from the following:

a headache   ~~toothache~~   a broken leg   a cut on my hand
a sore throat   a cold   burnt myself   stomach ache
a bad cough   a temperature

1   I've got ___*toothache*___ .

2   I've got _____

3   I've got _____

4   I've got _____

We can say: *I've got a broken leg.* OR *I've broken my leg.*
We can say: *I've got a cut on my hand.* OR *I've cut my hand.*
We can say: *I've got a burn on my hand.* OR *I've burnt my hand.*

5   I've got _____

6   I've got _____

7   I've got _____

8   I've got _____

9   I've got _____

10   I've _____

38 What are they saying? 2

Match the words to the pictures. Write the letters a to j in the balloons.

a   To eat here or take away?

b   Have you got the time, please?

c   Have a good trip.

d   Sleep well!

e   Good luck!

f   Congratulations!

g   Would you mind changing places with me?

h   Excuse me, is this seat free?

i   What's your job?

j   Goodbye. It was nice meeting you.

We don't just say *Congratulations* at weddings. We also say it when people pass an exam or get a new job.

39 In the kitchen

Write the numbers 1 to 19 next to the correct words.

cooker	_4_	fridge	____	plates	____
cupboard	____	frying pan	____	saucepan	____
cups	____	glasses	____	shelf	____
dishwasher	____	kettle	____	sink	____
drawer	____	knives	____	spoons	____
forks	____	microwave	____		
freezer	____	oven	____		

40 Sports and free time 1

Write the number of each picture next to the correct word. Then decide which of these verbs is correct for each activity: *go*, *do* or *play*.

____*do*____	athletics	3	_____	photography	☐
_____	chess	☐	_____	pottery	☐
_____	climbing	☐	_____	sailing	☐
_____	cycling	☐	_____	shopping	☐
_____	football	☐	_____	skiing	☐
_____	gymnastics	☐	_____	table tennis	☐

There's another test on sports and free time on page 64.

41 Choose the word

Write the missing word(s) in each sentence.

1   Yes, you're right. I agree _____*with*_____ you.

   a) to   (b) with   c) on

2   I _____ three years ago.

   a) stopped smoking   b) stopped to smoke
   c) finished smoking

3   I am _____ my brother to drive.

   a) learning   b) teaching   c) showing

4   Can you look _____ my cat next week? I'm going on holiday.

   a) at   b) after   c) for

5   I'm really looking forward _____ my holiday.

   a) with   b) to   c) against

6   Is there _____ for everyone?

   a) food enough   b) enough food   c) enough of food

7   _____ at the party on Saturday.

   a) We were fourteen   b) We were fourteen people

   c) There were fourteen of us

8   Don't go yet, I'm just going to _____ some coffee.

   a) make   b) cook   c) boil

9 She's got a very good _____ with a computer company.

a) work b) money c) job

10 The _____ from London to Edinburgh was quite tiring.

a) travel b) ticket c) journey

11 I'm afraid there isn't _____ in the car for everyone.

a) a room b) room c) the room

12 I can't see. Can you _____ with me?

a) change places b) change place c) change the place

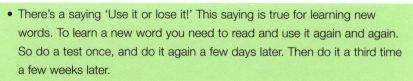

- There's a saying 'Use it or lose it!' This saying is true for learning new words. To learn a new word you need to read and use it again and again. So do a test once, and do it again a few days later. Then do it a third time a few weeks later.
- There are a lot of phrasal verbs with *look*: *look at, look for, look up, look after, look forward to, look out*. Try using each one in a sentence.

42 Irregular verbs crossword 1

In each sentence a verb is missing. Complete the crossword with the Past Simple of the correct verbs.

Across

Use these verbs for the Across clues.

> do   drive   give   have   leave   make   ~~meet~~   run   send   take

5 My sister ____*met*____ me at the airport.

6 We _____ him a computer game for his birthday.

8 Alex _____ me a beautiful postcard from India.

9 Mark _____ a delicious coffee cake yesterday.

12 I _____ breakfast in bed this morning.

14 We got in the car and _____ to the nearest beach.

16 She _____ to the station because she was late.

17 We _____ the party early because we were tired.

18 Who _____ all the washing-up?

19 It _____ me an hour to clean the oven last time.

Down

Use these verbs for the Down clues.

> buy   come   drink   fall   get   learn   read   say   shut   write

1 Martha _____ lots of new clothes last weekend.

2	We went by train and _____ home by bus.
3	They _____ married last summer.
4	He _____ a long letter to his favourite cousin.
7	She _____ quite a lot of Japanese when she went to Tokyo last year.
8	He _____ something really funny and we all laughed.
10	It was cold so I _____ all the windows.
11	I _____ off my chair because I was laughing so much.
13	I _____ lots of coffee last night and then I couldn't sleep.
15	I _____ something really interesting in a magazine last week.

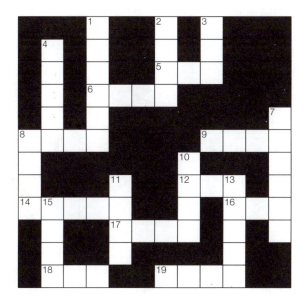

A lot of the commonest and most useful verbs are irregular in the Past Simple. So you really need to learn them!

43 Sports and free time 2

Write the number of each picture next to the correct word. Then decide which of these verbs is correct for each activity: *go*, *do* or *play*.

play badminton	10	_____ ice-skating	☐
_____ baseball	☐	_____ karate	☐
_____ bowling	☐	_____ roller-blading	☐
_____ computer games	☐	_____ tennis	☐
_____ golf	☐	_____ windsurfing	☐
_____ horse-riding	☐	_____ yoga	☐

A lot of people find it easier to learn new words in a *set*. On this page you have learnt a set of sports words. Can you add any more words to it?

44 Let's get technical

In each sentence replace the word(s) in **darker type** with the correct word(s) from one of the other sentences.

mouse

1   Move the ~~CD~~ on the table then click on the left to open a new window.

2   I can't do my Maths. Please lend me your **microwave** for a minute.

3   I don't wear glasses. I've got **headphones** now.

4   I need to get some new **contact lenses** for my personal stereo. These ones are dead.

5   Cindy's got lots of really exciting computer **batteries**. Let's go and play one.

6   Put the soup in the **computer** and it will be hot in thirty seconds.

7   Do you want to listen to the new Madonna ~~mouse~~? *CD*

8   Take the **remote control** with you. Then I can call you while you're at the shops.

9   My teacher can't read my handwriting so I always do my homework on a **mobile phone**.

10 There's a problem with my **games**. I can't hear anything through the left one.

11 Where's the **calculator**? I want to change the TV programme.

- The word *mouse* has two meanings: something you use with a computer, and a little animal with a long tail. Which meaning did you learn first?

- Make a list of English computer words used in your language.

- A *dead* battery doesn't work any more. We can also say a battery is *flat*.

45 Places in town 2

1   Where do you go to buy or do the things on the left? Choose from the
     places in the box.

bank   café   chemist's   dry-cleaner's   furniture shop   launderette
newsagent's   optician's   ~~shoe shop~~   supermarket   travel agent's

You want   **You go to a/an**

a   a pair of shoes
     or trainers      _shoe shop_

b   medicine,
     make-up   _____

c   potatoes, bread,
     batteries   _____

d   a newspaper, a magazine   _____

e   glasses, contact lenses   _____

f   to pay in a
     cheque   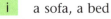   _____

g   to get your jacket or skirt cleaned   _____

h   to wash clothes   _____

i   a sofa, a bed   _____

j   a cup of tea, a sandwich   _____

k   to buy a
     plane ticket      _____

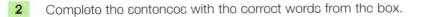

2 Complete the sentences with the correct words from the box.

> bookshop   church   library   mosque   music shop
> office   ~~police station~~

a Somebody has stolen my car. I have to go to the _police station_.

b Tara's got a new job. Her _____ is near my old school.

c You can borrow books, CDs, cassettes and videos at our

_____.

d Her grandparents go to St Paul's _____ every Sunday.

e I bought this dictionary at the new _____ in the

shopping centre.

f You can listen to CDs before you buy them in the

_____ near my house.

g Most of my Muslim friends go to the _____ near the

park.

- With many shop names, there is an apostrophe *s*: *optician's*,
  dry-cleaner's, *newsagent's*.
- Another word for a *chemist's* is a *pharmacy*.
- You borrow books at a library. If you want to buy books, you have to go
  to a bookshop.

46 Doing the housework and shopping

Write the numbers 1 to 12 next to the correct activities.

do the washing   _5_   do the cleaning ____

do the ironing   ____   make the beds   ____

do the cooking   ____   lay the table   ____

do the shopping   ____   clear the table ____

do the washing-up   ____   empty the bins ____

do the vacuuming   ____   tidy up   ____

- We *do* the cooking but we *make* lunch or supper.
  Who does the cooking in your family?
  I usually make supper but Chris makes lunch at the weekends.

- We also *make* a cake, a sandwich, a salad, coffee, spaghetti.
  Who made this cake? It's delicious!

47 Irregular verbs crossword 2

In each sentence a verb is missing. Complete the crossword with the Past Simple of the correct verbs.

Across

Use these verbs for the Across clues.

~~begin~~   break   cost   forget   hear   lend   lose
pay   ring   see   speak

1   I'm sorry I _____ your birthday.

3   We _____ the news on the radio last night.

5   Tony _____ me his calculator because mine was broken.

7   While you were out, somebody called Jim _____.

8   I _____ a snake in our garden last summer.

9   Her new trainers _____ about £50.

11 She _____ very quietly and nobody could hear her.

12 Liz sat on her glasses and _____ them.

13 I'm sorry you _____ the match last Saturday.

15 Who _____ the bill at the restaurant last night?

16 They _____ work at six this morning.

Down

Use these verbs for the Down clues.

choose   draw   feel   sell   sing   sleep   think   throw

1   I _____ ill this morning so I stayed in bed.

2 When you were away, I _____ about you all the time.

4 Who _____ glasses and a hat on this photo of me?

6 She _____ away all her old love letters.

9 The food was fantastic. I _____ the chicken with lemon.

10 I _____ until eleven o'clock this morning.

11 She needed money so she _____ all her CDs to me.

14 Steve _____ a Robbie Williams song at the school concert.

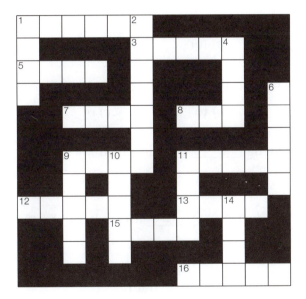

We form questions in the Past Simple with *did* and negatives with *didn't*.

Did you speak to Ginny last night?

What did you buy at the shops?

She didn't give me her address.

48 Prepositions 4 (mixed)

Write the missing prepositions in the following sentences.

1   I think Martina is afraid ____of____ dogs.

   a) for   (b) of   c) with

2   Andy, can I borrow a video _____ you this weekend?

   a) in   b) by   c) from

3   Can I pay _____ cheque, please?

   a) with   b) on   c) by

4   There's a café _____ the corner of West Street and Pond Road.

   a) on   b) for   c) from

5   Can you cut this photo out _____ your magazine?

   a) from   b) to   c) of

6   Dorota's living _____ a girl called Michelle.

   a) at   b) by   c) with

7   Look at the exercise _____ the bottom of page 17.

   a) on   b) at   c) in

8   We went to Paris _____ train.

   a) by   b) with the   c) on

9   I usually have a little party _____ my birthday.

   a) at   b) with   c) on

10 What time did you arrive _____ London?

    a) at   b) in   c) to

11 There's a bus stop _____ the end of the road.

    a) at   b) in   c) to

12 They've got a big flat _____ the centre of Paris.

    a) on   b) in   c) at

- We can say *scared of* instead of *afraid of*.
  I'm scared of dogs.
  She's scared of walking home in the dark.
- Another word for *scared* is *frightened*.

49 Word association

Next to each word on the left, write the word from the box that goes best with it. Use each word once only.

1	letter	*envelope*	motorway
2	railway station	_____	cassette
3	fruit salad	_____	toothache
4	knife	_____	teachers
5	sky	_____	fork
6	house	_____	garden
7	car	_____	ice cream
8	school	_____	game
9	husband	_____	comb
10	computer	_____	coffee
11	personal stereo	_____	wife
12	hair	_____	bridge
13	dentist	_____	cloud
14	cup	_____	train
15	river	_____	~~envelope~~

- **Question:** What eight-letter word has only got one letter in it?
  Answer: Envelope.
- Think about this problem. Most people forget 80% of new information in 24 hours. In a week, most of us forget another 10%.
  What can you do about it? After doing a test, ask yourself, 'What new words did I learn?' Make a list of them. The next day, look at the new words again. Look at them a third time one week later.

50 Pets and other animals

Write the numbers 1 to 20 next to the correct words.

a budgie __5__   a dog _____   a mouse _____   a rat _____

a bull _____   a duck _____   a parrot _____   a sheep _____

a cat _____   a goat _____   a pig _____   a snake _____

a chicken _____   a goldfish _____   a puppy _____   a spider _____

a cow _____   a kitten _____   a rabbit _____   a worm _____

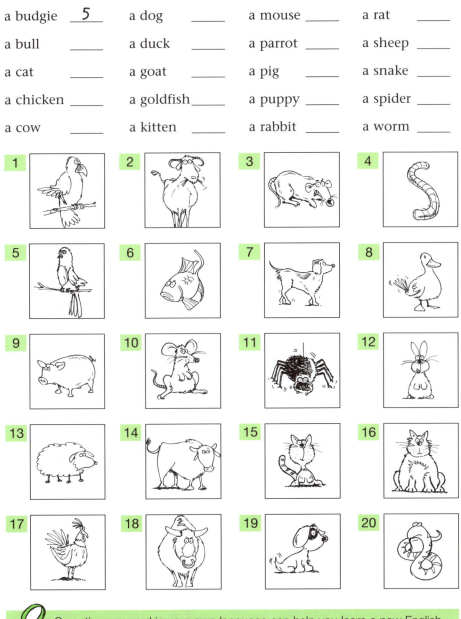

Sometimes a word in your own language can help you learn a new English word. For example, the English word *rabbit* sounds a bit like the Moroccan town, Rabat. An Arabic speaker can think of a rabbit in Rabat.

51 What kind of things are they?

Choose the correct word from the box to end each sentence. Use each word once only.

---

boys' names   buildings   capital cities   clothes   colours
countries   fruits   furniture   girls' names   ~~meals~~
meals outside   months   musical instruments   numbers
pets   relatives   rivers   sports   vegetables   wild animals

---

1 Breakfast and lunch are _____*meals*_____

2 Baseball and rugby are _____

3 Finland and New Zealand are _____

4 A table and a sofa are _____

5 A guitar and a piano are _____

6 A cousin and an aunt are _____

7 A sweater and a shirt are _____

8 Helen and Claudia are _____

9 Beans and onions are _____

10 Orange and purple are _____

11 Eighteen and thirty are _____

12 The Amazon and the Nile are _____

13 Peter and Mark are _____

14 A cat and a dog are _____

15 Madrid and Copenhagen are _____

16 March and July are _____

17 A lion and an elephant are _____

18 A hotel and a supermarket are _____

19 A pear and a pineapple are _____

20 A barbecue and a picnic are _____

You can often guess the meaning of a word. For example, in this test, you know that *a lion* and *an elephant* aren't *pets*. So they must be *wild animals*. Perhaps you don't know the word *wild*. But you can guess it means *animals that aren't pets*. Guessing the meaning of words can make learning quicker and more fun.

52 Crossword: It rhymes with ...

Complete the crossword using the clues.

Across

1 Windows are made of this. It rhymes with **class**.

4 This month rhymes with **sky**.

6 You eat it for breakfast. It rhymes with **post**.

9 A small animal with eight legs. It rhymes with **wider**.

10 You do this at night. It rhymes with **cheap**.

12 You wear them. They rhyme with **whose**.

15 A colour. It rhymes with **bed**.

17 A vegetable. It rhymes with **parrot**.

18 It's on your face and rhymes with **shows**.

19 The opposite of day. It rhymes with **write**.

Down

1 You wear them to see better. They rhyme with **passes**.

2 The opposite of north. It rhymes with **mouth**.

3 This pet rhymes with **hat**.

5 You drive it. It rhymes with **sorry**.

7 This game for two people rhymes with **less**.

8 It's very hot. It rhymes with **higher**.

11 It's a fruit. It rhymes with **where**.

12 The opposite of happy. It rhymes with **bad**.

13 It comes after winter. It rhymes with **sing**.

14 A country. It rhymes with **rain**.

16 A number. It rhymes with **gate**.

Rhymes can help you remember words. Is the word *funny* difficult to remember? Think of another word you know with almost the same sound, like *money*. Then think of a person holding a lot of money and laughing. Money = funny!

53 One to go

In each group of words on the left, one word shouldn't be there. Underline it and write it in the correct sentence on the right.

1	Monday, Thursday, <u>July</u>, Friday	a	_____ isn't a colour.
2	bright, yellow, orange, green	b	_July_ isn't a day of the week.
3	banana, apple, onion, pear	c	_____ is a nationality not a country.
4	cat, dog, horse, parrot	d	_____ isn't a number.
5	sofa, coat, table, chair	e	_____ isn't a sport.
6	lemon, carrot, onion, potato	f	A _____ goes on the water.
7	seven, thirty, eighteen, once	g	You don't use a _____ to eat.
8	Belgian, Denmark, Brazil, Japan	h	A _____ isn't a building.
9	spoon, knife, cup, fork	i	A _____ isn't a vegetable.
10	brother, niece, grandfather, uncle	j	You don't wear a _____ on your head.
11	car, bus, ship, lorry	k	A _____ isn't furniture.
12	cheese, bread, sausages, coffee	l	An _____ isn't a fruit.
13	photography, rugby, skiing, tennis	m	You can't drink _____.
14	milk, water, tea, petrol	n	You don't eat _____.
15	post office, supermarket, park, hotel	o	A _____ is a girl, not a male.
16	cap, helmet, bag, hat	p	A _____ isn't a mammal.

Did you guess the meaning of the words *male* and *mammal*? How do you say these words in your language?

54 Words that sound the same

Some words in English have the same sound but different meanings. Read the questions and circle the correct answer.

1	Which is short for 'it is'?	(it's)	its
2	Which can you eat?	meat	meet
3	Which is half of four?	too	two
4	Which is a greeting?	high	hi
5	Which one is the place for a ship?	sea	see
6	Which is a fruit?	pear	pair
7	Which is short for 'they are'?	they're	there
8	Which is a door made of?	would	wood
9	Which has sixty minutes?	hour	our
10	Which is the opposite of 'old'?	knew	new
11	Which is the Past Simple of 'see'?	sore	saw
12	Which do you do with a pen?	write	right
13	Which is the number above seven?	ate	eight
14	Which is the Past Simple of 'throw'?	threw	through
15	Which is a vegetable?	bean	been

- The word *their* sounds the same as *they're* and *there*. We use it like this:
  'Have you got Tim and Sue's address?'
  'I've got their phone number but I haven't got their address.'

- **Man in restaurant:** Waiter, waiter! What is this?
  Waiter: It's bean soup.
  Man in restaurant: It's been soup, has it? Well what is it now?

55 Adjective + noun

Underline the best noun to go with each adjective.

1   an interesting (foot, <u>TV programme</u>, water)

2   a high (glass, suitcase, mountain)

3   a comfortable (chair, chicken, pencil)

4   a right (car, answer, umbrella)

5   a sunny (day, vegetable, student)

6   a noisy (party, ice cream, cup)

7   a married (child, woman, animal)

8   an empty (mobile phone, lemon, bottle)

9   a heavy (garden, river, bag)

10   a broken (window, banana, meal)

11   a loud (time, hotel, noise)

12   a wooden (tie, door, river)

13   a sharp (knife, book, table)

14   a long (radio, comb, walk)

15   a round (video, dog, ball)

16   a fast (car, shoe, kitchen)

17   a bright (smell, colour, taste)

18   an exciting (tomato, film, lamp)

19   a careful (soup, cassette, driver)

20   a happy (child, living room, cooker)

- The words *quick* and *fast* mean the same. But we say *a fast car*, NOT *a quick car*. We say *a quick answer*, NOT *a fast answer*.
- The word *fast* can be an adjective *It's a very fast car*, or an adverb *It goes fast*.

56 School subjects

Write the missing school subjects in the spaces. Choose from the following:

> Biology   Chemistry   English   French   Geography
> History   Maths   Physics

57 Choose the word

Write the missing word(s) in each sentence.

1 Turn on the ___light___ , please. It's very dark in here.

   a) light   b) lighter   c) matches

2 I usually have a boiled _____ for breakfast.

   a) egg   b) plate   c) coffee

3 Her work is very good. She makes _____ mistakes.

   a) any   b) hardly any   c) a little

4 We usually _____ television in the evenings.

   a) watch   b) look   c) see

5 After running 800 metres, Carly felt really _____.

   a) angry   b) tired   c) friendly

6 Tom and Chris were born on the same day. They are _____.

   a) twins   b) pairs   c) partners

7 Anne is very good _____ tennis.

   a) at   b) with   c) in

8 I feel _____. I think I'll make myself a sandwich.

   a) hungry   b) thirsty   c) angry

9 We _____ the last bus home.

   a) rode   b) caught   c) travelled by

10 Hello. _____ Josie speaking.

   a) I am   b) Here is   c) This is

58 Six-letter words

Read the clues and fill in the two missing letters in each word.

Clues

1. You go there to see a film.
2. You take this on holiday for photographs.

| C | I | N | E | M | A |
| □ | A | M | E | R | □ |

3. A popular sport.
4. Most rooms in a house have at least one.

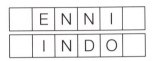

| □ | E | N | N | I | □ |
| □ | I | N | D | O | □ |

5. Your brother's son.
6. The opposite of the past.
7. A phone that you carry everywhere.
8. You walk on it in a room.
9. You can buy water in a plastic or glass one.

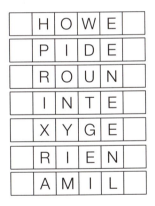

□	E	P	H	E	□
□	U	T	U	R	□
□	O	B	I	L	□
□	A	R	P	E	□
□	O	T	T	L	□

10. You use it in the bathroom.
11. A small animal with eight legs.
12. We stand on it outside.
13. The coldest time of year.
14. What everybody breathes.
15. Somebody you like a lot.
16. Your parents, children, husband, wife, etc.

□	H	O	W	E	□
□	P	I	D	E	□
□	R	O	U	N	□
□	I	N	T	E	□
□	X	Y	G	E	□
□	R	I	E	N	□
□	A	M	I	L	□

17. A musical instrument with four strings.

| □ | I | O | L | I | □ |

18. A fruit and a colour.
19. A mother or a father.
20. You can pay for things with this.

□	R	A	N	G	□
□	A	R	E	N	□
□	H	E	Q	U	□

59 Two small words, one big word

Add a word from the box to the words below and make a bigger word.
Use the clues to help you.

> ache   ball   case   chair   club   cup   day
> fish   ~~man~~   paper   room   shake

Clues

1   post*man*___

He brings you
your letters.

2   suit_____

You put things in
it before you go
on holiday.

3   arm_____

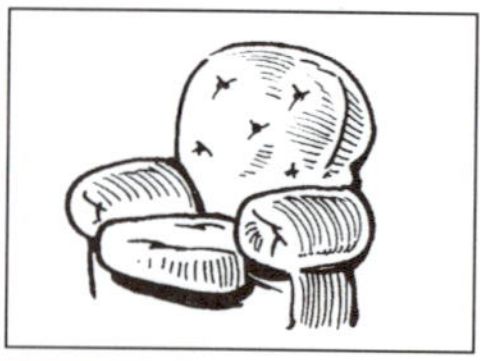

A comfortable
place to sit.

4   gold_____

This pet swims in
your home.

5   night_____

A place where
you can drink,
dance and listen
to music.

6	head_____		You feel bad when you've got one.
7	news_____		Lots of people read one every day.
8	tea_____		You drink out of it.
9	foot_____		A popular sport.
10	bed_____		Where most people sleep.
11	birth_____		You are one year older on this day.
12	milk_____		A drink. It can be a chocolate or banana one, for example.

60 Where are they?

Where were these people speaking? Match their words to the places.

at a football match	_____	at the cinema	_____
at a post office	_____	at a hotel	_____
at the doctor's	_____	in a computer shop	_____
at a newsagent's	_1_	in a lift	_____
on a plane	_____	at a chemist's	_____
at a hairdresser's	_____	in a shoe shop	_____
inside a car	_____	on the beach	_____
at a party on 31st December	_____	in a library	_____

1
'The Times' and 'Hello!' magazine, please.

2
I'd like to send this to Australia, please.

3
This is your captain speaking.

4
Come on, you Reds!

5
Have you got anything for a bad cold?

6
Have you got these trainers in black – size 8?

7 Let's go for a swim.

8 Happy New Year!

9 Where are the photography books?

10 Which floor do you want?

11 I've got stomach ache.

12 Have you got a double room with a bathroom, please?

13 Have you got a mouse, please?

14 You're driving too fast!

15 Two tickets for the James Bond film, please.

16 Don't cut too much off the front, please.

Answers

Test 1
1 dance
2 sing
3 sleep
4 swim
5 listen
6 drive
7 cry
8 write
9 laugh
10 drink
11 read
12 run
13 want
14 study
15 put

Test 2
1 bad
2 thin
3 small
4 short
5 empty
6 old
7 closed
8 poor
9 cold
10 new
11 sad
12 slow
13 low
14 dry
15 soft

Test 3
arm 12
back 3
bottom 2
ear 5
eye 8
foot 15
hair 6
hand 13
head 7
knee 14
leg 1
mouth 11
neck 4
nose 9
teeth 10

Test 4
1 in
2 between
3 on
4 in front of
5 behind
6 over
7 under
8 next to
9 through

Test 5
1 phone
2 fly
3 open
4 watch
5 learn
6 smoke
7 carry
8 sit down
9 wash
10 ask
11 play
12 eat
13 kick
14 happen
15 hurt

Test 6
a banana 1
bread 8
cheese 10
a cup of tea 5
fruit 3
an ice cream 12
jam 6
oranges 2
sausages 4
toast 7
vegetables 9
wine 11

Test 7
1
a) Theresa/Alan
b) Craig/Emily
c) Rebecca
d) Michael
e) Charlotte/John
f) Freddie
g) Lizzie/Vicky
h) Stephen
i) Sylvia

2
a) son
b) grandson
c) uncle
d) nieces
e) nephews
f) wife
g) mother
h) husband
i) aunt
j) sisters
k) cousin
l) daughter
m) parents
n) grandmother
o) grandfather
p) grandchildren
q) granddaughter

Test 8
1 come
2 know
3 walk
4 tell
5 wear
6 spell
7 Shut
8 climb
9 sell
10 cook
11 find
12 visit
13 give
14 keep
15 forget

Test 9
1 boring
2 stupid
3 expensive
4 wrong
5 noisy
6 light
7 difficult
8 late
9 dangerous
10 awake
11 dirty

12 deep
13 unfriendly
14 ugly
15 unkind
Sentence in darker
squares: *Opposites are
fun.*

Test 10
Across
 1 Russian
 3 Germany
 4 Poland
 7 Norwegian
 8 Brazil
 9 Turkish
10 Chinese
12 French
14 American
16 Switzerland
17 Denmark
18 Swedish

Down
 2 Spain
 3 Greek
 5 Japanese
 6 Portuguese
 8 Britain
11 Italy
13 Holland
15 Indian

Test 11
actor 8
dentist 5
doctor 2
driver 6
hairdresser 1
journalist 7
receptionist 3
waiter 4

Test 12
 1a) tall
 2b) can speak
 3a) were born
 4b) is
 5a) some
 6c) far
 7c) I'm sorry
 8a) Everyone

 9a) get up
10c) ill

Test 13
 1 cries
 2 hears
 3 leave
 4 speaks
 5 look at
 6 counts
 7 finishes
 8 copies
 9 helps
10 draws
11 lose
12 understand
13 kills
14 has
15 tries

Test 14
 1 It's freezing.
 2 It's foggy.
 3 It's raining.
 4 It's cloudy.
 5 It's stormy.
 6 It's windy.
 7 It's sunny.
 8 It's snowing.

Test 15
1

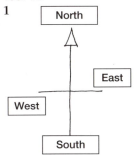

The Rainbow Mountains
The Murupara Forest
Cook Airport
The Clarence River
Wellington Road
Wellington Bridge
The Coral Sea
Blue Water Beach
Rabbit Island

2
Wellington C
Makogai A
Fulaga E
Nacula D
Yasawa B

Test 16
beautician 1
cleaner 6
electrician 4
optician 8
photographer 7
plumber 2
sales assistant 5
teacher 3

Test 17
Across
 1 potatoes
 3 mice
 6 feet
 8 men
 9 children
10 kisses
11 babies
13 taxis
14 glasses

Down
 2 teeth
 4 countries
 5 women
 7 knives
 9 cities
11 boxes
12 buses

Test 18
apples 3
beer 10
biscuits 8
a boiled egg 1
butter 12
a cake 11
a cup of coffee 9
meat 2
pears 4
potatoes 6
soup 7
tomatoes 5

Test 19

1 at	7 at
2 on	8 in
3 for	9 in
4 at, in	10 for, in
5 at	11 in
6 on	12 on

Test 20

1

a) start
b) cry
c) close
d) go
e) play
f) take
g) teach
h) borrow
i) turn off
j) answer
k) hate
l) buy
m) push
n) stand up
o) leave

2

a) teach
b) bring
c) pull
d) learn
e) sell
f) turn off
g) start
h) hate

Test 21

1(e) Hold on, please.
2(a) After you!
3(f) Bless you!
4(j) I'm terribly sorry!
5(d) Excuse me, please.
6(g) Take a seat.
7(i) Cheers!
8(h) Help yourselves.
9(c) Nice to meet you.
10(b) Watch out!

Test 22

1 rained
2 cleaned
3 moved
4 showed
5 talked
6 jumped
7 called
8 invited
9 needed
10 enjoyed
11 cried
12 stopped
13 used
14 waited
15 planned

Test 23

beans 4
chicken 3
fish and chips 2
a fried egg 9
a glass of milk 6
a hamburger 5
a hot dog 12
a lemon 11
a pizza 10
a sandwich 8
spaghetti 7
strawberries 1

Test 24

1a) There's
2a) am going
3c) work
4a) Pass
5c) well
6a) comes with
7b) a swim
8c) That's all right.
9b) change
10a) a piece of bread

Test 25

1 tomorrow
2 yesterday
3 next Thursday
4 tonight
5 the day after
   tomorrow
6 tomorrow afternoon
7 last Thursday
8 this afternoon
9 last night
10 this morning
11 the day before
   yesterday

Test 26

balcony 3
door 7
garage 8
garden 9
gate 11
grass 10
flowers 5
roof 1
steps 12
tree 2
wall 4
window 6

Test 27

1	**2**
a) take	a) go to
b) forget	sleep
c) die	b) get up
d) finish	c) drop
e) go to	d) remember
bed	e) whisper
f) save	f) save
g) mend	g) lose
h) take off	h) drop
i) lose	
j) pick up	
k) find	
l) hide	
m) go to	
sleep	
n) whisper	

Test 28

1 happy
2 hot
3 comfortable
4 frightened
5 cold
6 tired
7 sad
8 correct
9 embarrassed
10 ill
11 worried

Test 29

boots 17
bra 3
coat 12
dress 6
hat 13

jacket 10
jeans 16
knickers 5
pants 4
shirt 8
shoes 14
shorts 19
skirt 7
socks 1
suit 20
sweater 11
tie 9
tights 2
trainers 18
trousers 15

Test 30
block of flats 3
bridge 7
bus stop 4
café 1
car park 12
hospital 11
museum 2
park 6
railway station 10
school 5
supermarket 8
traffic lights 9

Test 31
1 rugby shirt
2 cycling helmet
3 football shorts
4 baseball cap
5 tennis skirt
6 ballet shoes
7 climbing boots
8 skiing hat

Test 32
bathroom 2
bedroom 7
dining-room 8
downstairs 9
hall 4
kitchen 6
living room 3
stairs 10
toilet 5
upstairs 1

Test 33
1c) at
2a) for
3b) at
4b) in
5c) with
6a) with
7b) on
8c) to
9c) from/for
10a) for
11b) for
12c) on

Test 34
1 nobody
2 country
3 bottom
4 single
5 always
6 worse
7 light
8 last
9 in front of
10 after
11 far
12 adult
13 future
14 hardly ever

Test 35
armchair 2
bookcase 5
carpet 6
CD player 12
clock 15
coffee table 4
cushion 16
light 8
magazines 9
picture 14
remote control 10
rug 7
sofa 3
television 1
vase of flowers 11
video recorder 13

Test 36
1 kiss
2 feel

3 recognize
4 pay
5 post
6 paint
7 change
8 smell
9 build
10 Smile
11 lie down
12 repeat
13 mean
14 stay
15 hope

Test 37
1 toothache
2 a headache
3 a broken leg
4 a cold
5 a sore throat
6 a cut on my hand
7 stomach ache
8 a bad cough
9 a temperature
10 burnt myself

Test 38
1(f) Congratulations!
2(h)Excuse me, is this
    seat free?
3(d)Sleep well!
4(g)Would you mind
    changing places
    with me?
5(c) Have a good trip.
6(a)To eat here or take
    away?
7(b)Have you got the
    time, please?
8(e) Good luck!
9(j) Goodbye. It was
    nice meeting you.
10(i) What's your job?

Test 39
cooker 4
cupboard 11
cups 16
dishwasher 7
drawer 19
forks 10

freezer 6
fridge 17
frying pan 2
glasses 8
kettle 12
knives 1
microwave 15
oven 9
plates 3
saucepan 13
shelf 18
sink 5
spoons 14

Test 40

do athletics 3
play chess 2
go climbing 4
go cycling 8
play football 6
do gymnastics 7
do photography 10
do pottery 1
go sailing 11
go shopping 12
go skiing 9
play table tennis 5

Test 41

1b) with
2a) stopped
    smoking
3b) teaching
4b) after
5b) to
6b) enough food
7c) There were
    fourteen of us
8a) make
9c) job
10c) journey
11b) room
12a) change places

Test 42

Across
5 met
6 gave
8 sent
9 made
12 had
14 drove

16 ran
17 left
18 did
19 took

Down
1 bought
2 came
3 got
4 wrote
7 learnt
8 said
10 shut
11 fell
13 drank
15 read

Test 43

play badminton 10
play baseball 4
go bowling 9
play computer games 2
play golf 6
go horse-riding 7
go ice-skating 3
do karate 8
go roller-blading 11
play tennis 12
go windsurfing 1
do yoga 5

Test 44

1 mouse
2 calculator
3 contact lenses
4 batteries
5 games
6 microwave
7 CD
8 mobile phone
9 computer
10 headphones
11 remote control

Test 45

1
a) shoe shop
b) chemist's
c) supermarket
d) newsagent's
e) optician's
f) bank

g) dry-cleaner's
h) launderette
i) furniture shop
j) café
k) travel agent's

2
a) police station
b) office
c) library
d) church
e) bookshop
f) music shop
g) mosque

Test 46

do the washing 5
do the ironing 7
do the cooking 11
do the shopping 9
do the washing-up 2
do the vacuuming 10
do the cleaning 8
make the beds 1
lay the table 6
clear the table 12
empty the bins 3
tidy up 4

Test 47

Across
1 forgot
3 heard
5 lent
7 rang
8 saw
9 cost
11 spoke
12 broke
13 lost
15 paid
16 began

Down
1 felt
2 thought
4 drew
6 threw
9 chose
10 slept
11 sold
14 sang

Test 48
1b) of
2c) from
3c) by
4a) on
5c) of
6c) with
7b) at
8a) by
9c) on
10b) in
11a) at
12b) in

Test 49
1 envelope
2 train
3 ice cream
4 fork
5 cloud
6 garden
7 motorway
8 teachers
9 wife
10 game
11 cassette
12 comb
13 toothache
14 coffee
15 bridge

Test 50
a budgie 5
a bull 18
a cat 16
a chicken 17
a cow 14
a dog 7
a duck 8
a goat 2
a goldfish 6
a kitten 15
a mouse 10
a parrot 1
a pig 9
a puppy 19
a rabbit 12
a rat 3
a sheep 13
a snake 20
a spider 11
a worm 4

Test 51
1 meals
2 sports
3 countries
4 furniture
5 musical instruments
6 relatives
7 clothes
8 girls' names
9 vegetables
10 colours
11 numbers
12 rivers
13 boys' names
14 pets
15 capital cities
16 months
17 wild animals
18 buildings
19 fruits
20 meals outside

Test 52
Across
1 glass
4 July
6 toast
9 spider
10 sleep
12 shoes
15 red
17 carrot
18 nose
19 night

Down
1 glasses
2 south
3 cat
5 lorry
7 chess
8 fire
11 pear
12 sad
13 spring
14 Spain
16 eight

Test 53
1(b) July isn't a day of the week.
2(a) Bright isn't a colour.
3(l) An onion isn't a fruit.
4(p) A parrot isn't a mammal.
5(k) A coat isn't furniture.
6(i) A lemon isn't a vegetable.
7(d) Once isn't a number.
8(c) Belgian is a nationality not a country.
9(g) You don't use a cup to eat.
10(o) A niece is a girl, not a male.
11(f) A ship goes on the water.
12(n) You don't eat coffee.
13(e) Photography isn't a sport.
14(m) You can't drink petrol.
15(h) A park isn't a building.
16(j) You don't wear a bag on your head.

Test 54
1 it's
2 meat
3 two
4 hi
5 sea
6 pear
7 they're
8 wood
9 hour
10 new
11 saw
12 write
13 eight
14 threw
15 bean

Test 55
1 TV programme
2 mountain
3 chair
4 answer
5 day

6 party
7 woman
8 bottle
9 bag
10 window
11 noise
12 door
13 knife
14 walk
15 ball
16 car
17 colour
18 film
19 driver
20 child

Test 56
1 History
2 Maths
3 French
4 Geography
5 Biology
6 Chemistry
7 Physics
8 English

Test 57
1a) light
2a) egg
3b) hardly any
4a) watch

5b) tired
6a) twins
7a) at
8a) hungry
9b) caught
10c) This is

Test 58
1 cinema
2 camera
3 tennis
4 window
5 nephew
6 future
7 mobile
8 carpet
9 bottle
10 shower
11 spider
12 ground
13 winter
14 oxygen
15 friend
16 family
17 violin
18 orange
19 parent
20 cheque

Test 59
1 postman

2 suitcase
3 armchair
4 goldfish
5 night club
6 headache
7 newspaper
8 teacup
9 football
10 bedroom
11 birthday
12 milkshake

Test 60
at a football match 4
at a post office 2
at the doctor's 11
at a newsagent's 1
on a plane 3
at a hairdresser's 16
inside a car 14
at a party on 31st
    December 8
at the cinema 15
at a hotel 12
in a computer shop 13
in a lift 10
at a chemist's 5
in a shoe shop 6
on the beach 7
in a library 9

Word list

The numbers after the entries are the tests in which they appear.

A
actor 11
after 34
afternoon 25
airport 15
always 34
American 10
answer 20
apples 18
arm 3
armchair 35
arrive 20
ask 5
asleep 9
at 19
athletics 40
aunt 7
awake 9

B
babies 17
back 3
bad 2
badminton 43
bag 53
balcony 26
ball 55
ballet 31
banana 6
bank 45
baseball 31
bathroom 32
batteries 44
beach 15
beans 23
beautician 16
bedroom 32
beer 18
begin 27
behind 4
Belgian 53
between 4
big 2
bins 46
Biology 56
birthday 59
biscuits 18
block of flats 30
boiled 18
bookcase 35
bookshop 45
boots 29
boring 9

borrow 20
bottle 55
bottom 3
bowling 43
boxes 17
bra 29
Brazil 10
bread 6
break 27
bridge 15
bright 53
bring 20
Britain 10
broken 37
budgie 50
build 36
buildings 51
bull 50
burn 37
bus stop 30
buses 17
butter 18
buy 20
by 48

C
café 30
cake 18
calculator 44
call 22
camera 58
cap 31
capital cities 51
car 49
car park 30
carpet 35
carrot 52
carry 5
cassette 49
cat 50
CD 44
CD player 35
chair 55
change (n) 24
change (v) 36
cheap 9
cheese 6
chemist 45
Chemistry 56
cheque 58
chess 40
chicken 23
child 55

children 17
Chinese 10
choose 47
church 45
cinema 58
cities 17
clean 9
cleaner 16
cleaning 46
clear 46
clever 9
climb 8
climbing 31
close 20
closed 2
clothes 51
cloud 49
cloudy 14
coat 29
coffee 18
cold (adj) 2
cold (n) 37
colours 51
comb 49
come 8
comfortable 28
computer 44
computer games 43
contact lenses 44
cook 8
cooker 39
cooking 46
copy 13
correct 28
cost 47
cough 37
count 13
countries 17
cousin 7
cow 50
cry 1
cup 6
cupboard 39
cushion 35
cut 37
cycling 31

D
dance 1
dangerous 9
daughter 7
day 55
deep 9
Denmark 10
dentist 11
die 27
difficult 9
dining-room 32
dirty 9

dishwasher 39
do 42
doctor 11
dog 50
door 26
downstairs 32
draw 13
drawer 39
dress 29
drink 1
drive 1
driver 11
dry 2
dry-cleaner 45
duck 50

E
ear 3
early 9
east 15
easy 9
eat 5
egg 18
eight 52
electrician 16
embarrassed 28
empty (adj) 2
empty (v) 46
English 56
enjoy 22
enough 41
envelope 49
everyone 12
expensive 9
eye 3

F
fall 42
family 58
far 12
fast 2
fat 2
feel 36
feet 17
film 55
find 8
finish 13
fire 52
fish and chips 23
flowers 26
fly 5
foggy 14
food 41
foot 3
football 31
football match 60
for 19
forest 15
forget 8

forks 39
freezer 39
freezing 14
French 10
fridge 39
fried 23
friend 58
friendly 9
frightened 28
from 33
fruit 6
fruit salad 49
frying pan 39
full 2
furniture 45
future 34

G
garage 26
garden 26
gate 26
Geography 56
Germany 10
get 42
get up 12
give 8
glass 52
glasses 17
go 20
goat 50
goldfish 50
golf 43
good 2
grandchildren 7
granddaughter 7
grandfather 7
grandmother 7
grandson 7
grass 26
Greek 10
ground 58
gymnastics 40

H
hair 3
hairdresser 11
hall 32
hamburger 23
hand 3
happen 5
happy 2
hard 2
hardly any 57
hardly ever 34
hat 29
hate 20
have 13
head 3
headache 37

headphones 44
hear 13
heavy 9
helmet 31
help 13
hi 54
hide 27
high 2
History 56
Holland 10
hope 36
horse-riding 43
hospital 30
hot 2
hot dog 23
hotel 60
hour 54
house 49
hungry 57
hurt 5
husband 7

I
ice cream 6
ice-skating 43
ill 12
in 4
in front of 4
Indian 10
interesting 9
invite 22
ironing 46
island 15
Italy 10
it's 54

J
jacket 29
jam 6
Japanese 10
jeans 29
job 41
journalist 11
journey 41
July 52
jump 22

K
karate 43
keep 8
kettle 39
kick 5
kill 13
kind 9
kiss (v) 36
kisses 17
kitchen 32
kitten 50
knee 3
knickers 29

Portuguese 10
post 36
post office 60
postman 59
potatoes 17
pottery 40
pretty 9
pull 20
puppy 50
push 20
put 1
put on 27

Q
quiet 9

R
rabbit 50
railway station 30
rain 22
raining 14
rat 50
read 1
receptionist 11
recognize 36
red 52
relatives 51
remember 27
remote control 35
repeat 36
rich 2
right 9
ring 47
river 15
road 15
roller-blading 43
roof 26
room 41
rug 35
rugby 31
run 1
Russian 10

S
sad 28
sailing 40
sales assistant 16
sandwich 23
saucepan 39
sausages 6
save 27
say 42
school 30
sea 15
see 47
sell 8
send 42
shallow 9
sheep 50
shelf 39

ship 53
shirt 29
shoe shop 45
shoes 29
shopping 40
short 2
shorts 29
shout 27
show 22
shower 58
shut 8
sing 1
single 34
sink 39
sister 7
sit down 5
skiing 31
skirt 29
sky 49
sleep 1
slow 2
small 2
smell 36
smile 36
smoke 5
smoking 41
snake 47
snowing 14
socks 29
sofa 35
soft 2
some 12
son 7
sore throat 37
sorry 12
soup 18
south 15
spaghetti 23
Spain 10
speak 12
spell 8
spend 27
spider 50
spoons 39
sports 51
spring 52
stairs 32
stand up 20
start 20
stay 36
steps 26
stomach ache 37
stop 20
stormy 14
strawberries 23
study 1
stupid 9
suit 29

Test Your way to success in English
Test Your Vocabulary

0582 45166 3

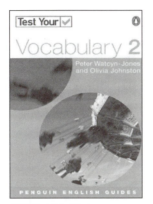

0582 45167 1

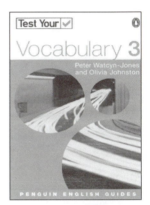

0582 45168 X

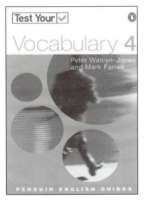

0582 45169 8

0582 45170 1

Test Your way to success in English
Test Your Grammar and Skills

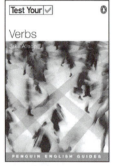

0582 45176 0

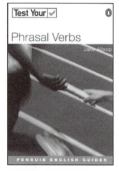

0582 45171 X

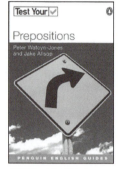

0582 45172 8

0582 45173 6

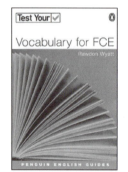

0582 45175 2

0582 45174 4

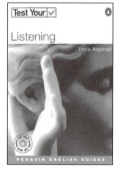

0582 46902 3

0582 46908 2

0582 46905 8

Test Your way to success in English

Test Your Professional English

Test Your ✓ | Ⓟ
Professional English
Accounting
Alison Pohl
Series Editor: Nick Brieger
PENGUIN ENGLISH GUIDES

0582 45163 9

Test Your ✓ | Ⓟ
Professional English
Business: General
Steve Flinders
Series Editor: Nick Brieger
PENGUIN ENGLISH GUIDES

0582 45148 5

Test Your ✓ | Ⓟ
Professional English
Business: Intermediate
Steve Flinders
Series Editor: Nick Brieger
PENGUIN ENGLISH GUIDES

0582 45149 3

Test Your ✓ | Ⓟ
Professional English
Finance
Simon Sweeney
Series Editor: Nick Brieger
PENGUIN ENGLISH GUIDES

0582 45160 4

Test Your ✓ | Ⓟ
Professional English
Hotel and Catering
Alison Pohl
Series Editor: Nick Brieger
PENGUIN ENGLISH GUIDES

0582 45161 2

Test Your ✓ | Ⓟ
Professional English
Law
Nick Brieger
Series Editor: Nick Brieger
PENGUIN ENGLISH GUIDES

0582 46898 1

Test Your ✓ | Ⓟ
Professional English
Management
Simon Sweeney
Series Editor: Nick Brieger
PENGUIN ENGLISH GUIDES

0582 46897 3

Test Your ✓ | Ⓟ
Professional English
Marketing
Simon Sweeney
Series Editor: Nick Brieger
PENGUIN ENGLISH GUIDES

0582 45150 7

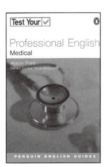

Test Your ✓ | Ⓟ
Professional English
Medical
Alison Pohl
Series Editor: Nick Brieger
PENGUIN ENGLISH GUIDES

0582 45147 7

Test Your ✓ | Ⓟ
Professional English
Secretarial
Alison Pohl
Series Editor: Nick Brieger
PENGUIN ENGLISH GUIDES

0582 45162 0

www.penguinenglish.com